Contact Information

Email: BeforeItsToooLate@hotmail.com

Instagram: Mr_Williamzz

Facebook: Mary-And-Terry Williams

The Walk Down the Aisle
https://youtu.be/_EosixANQ3A

Wedding Vows
https://youtu.be/YuDosaPpwsE

Our first dance
https://youtu.be/HQgk0aANNjc

When Terry met Mary (song)
https://youtu.be/2wUpfVfr1SA

The Most Beautifulest Girl in the world (Mary Bday Tribute)
https://youtu.be/cmUyJvrVfzU

Text or Call Me (951)816-1796

Dedication

I dedicate this book to my beautiful wife Mary Williams. You are my boo boo, my best friend, my lover and the missing piece to my puzzle which completes me. When I laid eyes on you for the first time I knew you were the one. I love you more than life itself. With these two eyes I seen and met tons of females but **NONE OF THEM EVER MADE ME FEEL LIKE YOU.** Back then you were my dream, and you were my fantasy. When we said our wedding vows and sealed it with a kiss my fantasy became my reality. You are my Cinderella, you are my Juliet, you are my happily ever after and my dream come true. We been rockin together for the past 14 years, you're my wife and the mother of my kids and I will never ever stop adoring and cherishing you. You're my heartbeat, you're my backbone, you're my rib, and you are truly my world, **I LOVE YOU MI AMOR!!!!!!!**

Disclaimer: This book is intended for both husband and wife individually and or jointly. As I'm writing this book, I'm sharing my experiences from a husband's and man's perspective and point of view. But don't get it twisted wives and ladies, YES I SAID DONT GET IT TWISTED (lol) and the reason why is because even though I speak from a husband's and man's perspective, the wives can easily interchange the word 'husband' with the word 'wife' and instantly this book relates to the wives perspective and point of view as well.

Remember!!!!!

Husbands: Remember there was a reason why you got down on one knee and proposed.

Wives: Remember there was a reason why you said, "Yes" after he popped the question by proposing to you.

Husbands and Wives: Remember there was a reason why you both said
"I Do" and sealed it with a kiss at the altar.

My Wedding Proposal

Dear Future Wife!!!!!!!

I finally have the answers to my questions;
God sent you from heaven to me as a blessin'
But back then I didn't realize the revelation,
I was immature and the quest for sex was my only ambition;
Now with you all I'm seekin'
Is affection, passion, sharing of emotions,
And ending each night with a phone conversation.
Back then I used to constantly stare at your pictures,
Hoping your heart will be mine as I read these bible scriptures;
Every night I prayed that you will be mine,
And with strong faith in God I'll have you in due time.
Because Imma be obedient and patient,
And I don't care how long it takes I won't fall to temptation.
Again baby, we had a wonderful past,
But let's think about the future, edible thongs, hugs, laughs,
To rose petal bubble baths;
And Fa sho I'm going to suck your sexy toes,
But as the days goes, my love for you grows,

And lord knows,
I can't wait to get down on one knee and propose!!!!!!

The Dream and The Nightmare

The Dream

"Visions, thoughts, images come across the mind while you are asleep. It is pure perfection and satisfaction while you are in this state. The dream and the fantasy are so real that you don't want to wake up and go back to reality."

Let's rewind time and let's go WAAAAAY back. Erase all the thoughts of the current state of your marriage and take your mind back to the place where you were at the highest point of your marriage.

Husbands: She was your dream girl. When you first saw her and laid eyes on her she instantly caught your attention. You couldn't keep your eyes off of her and something about her intrigued you. There was nothing on this earth that was going to stop you from getting her contact information, so you can further communicate with her. The more you communicated with her the more you were drawn to her, the more you wanted her all to yourself and the more your eyes were only for her. Every little thing about her was beautiful to you. Every imperfection, every flaw she had you loved and adored. Out of all the women you ever dated in your life no one ever made you feel the way she made you feel. She made you want to be a better man. You thought about her every second of the day. Thoughts of her ran through your mind 24/7, and when you were at work you couldn't get home fast enough to be in her presence. She was the first thought on your mind when you woke up and the last thought on your mind when you went to sleep. When you were in dreamland you dreamed of her. If you woke up in the middle of the night you would see her laying in bed so sexy in her pajamas, that you couldn't resist snuggling close to her, hugging her tight and kissing her shoulders before dozing back off to sleep.

No other female on this earth mattered to you, because to you she was your everything. All the failed relationships you had in the past, you took everything you learned, along with all the love that you had and pumped it all into her. She was your queen. You laughed with her, joked with her and bonded with her on all levels. With no doubt in your heart, you felt she was the one. You got down on one knee, you said some sweet words that came from your soul, then you asked her to marry you. You asked her to spend the rest of her life with you, while putting a ring on her finger.

   You were so ready for her to share your world by giving her your last name because she completed you. She was your heartbeat, she was your rib, and she was the oxygen you needed to keep you alive. You felt without her in your life, you would be incomplete because she was the missing piece to your puzzle. You gave her the world. She was your world, so everything in your world you gave to her. You gave her the most precious, the most sensitive and the most protected gift a man could give a woman. Which was your WHOLE heart and ALL of the love in it. She was everything you ever wanted in a woman, she was your baby girl and she could do no wrong in your eyes.

   Even before you asked her to marry you, you knew she was special. You wined and dined her, catered to her and were very patient with her. You fulfilled and wanted to fulfill all of her needs mentally, emotionally, physically and sexually. You made sure you fulfilled her every want, every need and every desire. When you put it down in the bedroom, you let her know that she was all yours, taking your time with her, giving her the perfect mixture of lovemaking and freakiness. When you took her on a date you made sure you were dressed to impress, looking fly, fresh and smooth because she brought out the best in you. You got your haircut weekly, so you can always stay fresh just in case she wanted to see you spontaneously.

When you kissed her lips and let your tongue massage hers, there was MEANING and PASSION behind it. You treated every kiss, every hug, and every time you made love with her, like it was your last day on this earth. She was everything you could ever ask for in a woman, your best friend, your lover, your personal freak, your soulmate and your wife all in one.

Wives: He was the man of your dreams. He brought you confidence, made you feel secure and protected in every way, shape and form. He stimulated your mind, captured your attention and sparked your curiosity before you were even officially his. But every time you spoke or texted, you knew in your heart you wanted to be his one and only. Your eyes were only for him.

When different men would flirt with you or ask you out on dates you wouldn't entertain any of them, because in your world and in your heart no other man could compare to him. When he would take you to dinner, you made sure your hair and makeup was 'on point' because you wanted to look good on his arm. You wanted to look delicious on his arm and you wanted every female that saw him with you by his side to know that he was off limits. You wanted to look beautiful and sexy for him at all times and even though you heard it from different men, it just meant so much more when he would look at you passionately and would say in his voice "you look so beautiful and sexy". That meant the world to you coming from him because he noticed.

Your world revolved around his and you made sure he knew that by trusting his words and trusting his heart. Your heart beats his name. Out of all the failed relationships you had and the broken hearts you received, something about this man made you want to give relationships and a shot at love another chance. You loved all of his flaws and imperfections because all of his flaws and imperfections made him who he is. You love who he is, so his flaws and imperfections made him perfect in your eyes.

When his lips touched yours and his tongue slow danced with yours, you could feel the love and passion he had for you. You wanted to help him fulfill all of his dreams, desires, and satisfy all of his needs. You wanted to be there for him and connect with him in ways no other female had ever been. All you ever wanted was a man to love you, be in love with you, to protect your heart, cherish you and give you the assurance that you are all that he needs. You love him because he gives you all that and more.

You felt like the luckiest woman in the world when he proposed. You picked out the most beautiful white dress you could find so you could look good for your man. You wore his last name with pride. When he was sick your love was his medicine. You looked out for him, protected him and gave him strength by believing in his dreams. You were his earthly guardian angel. You were also his bedroom angel. Your main goal was to please your husband by not holding anything back. All the insecurities you may have had about your body weren't insecurities anymore, because his love gave you confidence, which in return made you feel secure.

You had the right balance of lovemaking and being freaky which drove him crazy. You delivered all that passion, fire, and desire to your husband. You were his best friend, lover, freak, wife, and soulmate. He was the missing piece to your puzzle.

The Nightmare

"When you are in a sleep state and the unthinkable is happening. Every vision, every thought is frightening and difficult to deal with. During the sleep state you are constantly tossing and turning begging to wake up and when you awake you say to yourself, "Wow, that felt so real."

Husbands: Imagine another man feeling the same way that you once felt about your wife. Imagine another man seeing and appreciating the outer and inner beauty that you once saw in your wife. Imagine another man loving your wife with so much passion and so much intensity like you once did. Imagine another man getting his heart broken and done dirty by a female from his past and the next female he met was your wife. Imagine another man bonding, laughing, joking, and having so much chemistry with your wife like you once shared. Imagine another man wining and dining your wife like you once did. Imagine another man hugging your wife and kissing your wife with so much passion like you once did. Imagine another man fulfilling all of your wife's fantasies, desires, wants and needs like you once did. Imagine another man making love to your wife with all of his heart, letting her know that there is no rush and that he wants to take his time while he is pleasing her like you once did.

Imagine another man seeing what you once saw in your wife. Imagine another man giving your wife his all, giving her his heart and his love. Imagine another man feeling completed and feeling your wife is the missing piece to his puzzle that completes him like how you once felt.

*Put the book down for a moment, close your eyes and let the nightmare really sink into your mind and thoughts. This book isn't going anywhere. Don't even read anymore. Just let the nightmare take over your mind and heart. Put the book down and realize that this nightmare will be *reality depending on the decisions you make. Close the book and drown in your thoughts from the beautiful 'dream' you once had to the horrible 'nightmare' you will face.*

Wives: Imagine another woman loving your husband like you once did. Imagine another woman catering to your husband, cooking for him, fixing his favorite foods like you once did. Imagine another woman melting in your husband's arms like you once did. Imagine another woman going to the mall buying sexy clothes, so she can turn your husband on like you once did. Imagine another woman bragging to her friends that your husband is the man of her dreams like you once did. Imagine another woman believing in your husband and encouraging your husband to follow his dreams like you once did.

Imagine another woman receiving the 'I love you' text and the 'you're my world' text from your husband like you once received. Imagine another woman waiting in the bathtub for your husband to get home from work so they can just talk like you once did. Imagine another woman getting fulfilled mentally, and emotionally by your husband like you once did. Imagine another woman kissing your husband so passionately like you once did. Imagine another woman having a deep connection with your husband like you once had. Imagine another woman making love to your husband taking her time pleasing him, fulfilling all of his desires and needs like you once did.

Imagine another woman seeing the perfection in your husband like you once saw. Imagine another woman feeling like nothing else matters in this world but him like how you once felt. Imagine another woman feeling that your husband is her lover, best friend, soulmate and her world like how you once felt.

Put the book down take a deep breath and just breathe. Take it all in. Close your eyes and dwell on this nightmare. Really let this nightmare invade your thoughts and heart. Just lay in bed and think about the beautiful 'Dream' and think about the horrible 'Nightmare' which will be reality based upon your decisions.

Cuffing Season

"When a man or woman intrigues you, sparks your curiosity and interest more than anyone ever has. You pursue them differently than you ever pursued anyone before because, 'IT'S JUST SOMETHING' about that person. As you get to know the person you are so captivated by them that through your eyes everything about them is beautiful and perfect. And at that moment, you want to put the 'Boyfriend, Girlfriend' label on them, taking them off the dating market and making them exclusively yours. In other words, 'PUTTING THE HANDCUFFS ON THEM!'*

I first met Mary online back in 2004. I know you guys are saying, "OMG, LOL, WTF, you met your wife online?" LOL, yes I did. But I met her back in 2004 before online dating was even popular. Now that I am older, I'm glad I met her online rather than meeting her in a small city or in person. Meeting her online meant we were competing for each other's attention and hearts on a global scale. When I think about the odds, it's mind-blowing because out of thousands of girls' profiles I read and pictures I saw, I chose Mary. And on the flip side if you haven't seen Mary,

19

Mary is super hot, beautiful and sexy so I know she was receiving hundreds of messages daily from guys and she chose me. 😁

With that being said I'm not trying to pop my own collar, but I must be one cool dude, one special guy. I must be so fly I should have been born with wings. I must have been smoother than a baby's bottom and fresh like wet paint. Hahahahahaha lol rotfl. But back to my story. I saw her picture and I was like "Dayum baby is hot!" I then read her profile and it sparked my interest, so I decided to write her a message. The odds of her responding to me were slim because I knew dime pieces online get so many messages daily that they don't even read half of them. So once she responded that showed me she was mutually interested as well.

When I read her message I became more curious about her and super interested. I immediately had to stop myself from smiling so big and once I calmed down I had a one on one conversation with myself. I said "Terry stay focused. She's not even close to be being yours yet. There's tons of dudes writing her. Keep her interest, show her who Terry is, show her you're unique and a one of a kind dude. And most of all Terry don't F**k this up." I really didn't want to mess this up. So I did something I have never done with a female before and that was to take my time with her, be vulnerable, and be 100% real and transparent with her. And even though I was young, I wanted to come at her like how a grown man would.

That's when I set aside my boyish mentality and really showed myself and her the grown man I had become. That night we exchanged messages which led to our first phone conversation. When I called she picked up and said "Welcome to domino's pizza. May I help you?" me being the witty person I am I said, "I'll take a large pineapple pizza." We laughed and that phone conversation ended up lasting over four hours.

We had so much fun and so much chemistry that after our conversation ended, I hung up the phone saying to myself, "I need this. She has beauty and a cool personality." In my head I was 100% sure that other guys were hitting her up and trying to get with her. But as they were trying to get with her, I was getting to know her. There is a huge difference between getting with someone and getting to know someone.

So as the days went by and our conversation continued I was getting to know her, by studying her, listening to her, learning about her, applying what I was learning about her and taking my time with her. I was her laughter when she needed to laugh, and her ear when she needed someone to listen. When she wanted to talk about her day or just vent about something that was on her mind, I made sure she could depend on me. I was patient with her. When she needed consoling I was there. When we discussed past relationships and she talked about her heartbreaks, I was there to reassure her of her worth and I was there to put the broken pieces of her heart back together. I built a bond with her.

Before her all I wanted was a physical relationship with females. She was so beautiful to me on the inside and out, that I didn't rush and I trusted the process I was taking. I made love to her mind, made love to her heart and was fulfilling her emotional needs with each conversation we had. After a month of us just purely conversing through the phone, I felt it was time to meet Mary in person. Yes this whole time we never saw each other. *Side note* Mary was ready to see me and ready to meet the mystery man behind the phone conversations.

But I trusted the process, because I wanted to build a connection, and build something that was deeper than just the physical. So I stayed the course and decided not to see her until the time was right, which was now. On the way to pick up Mary for our first date, I was nervous. I was thinking this was the last step. The first step was we clicked online. The second step was our chemistry over the phone was undeniable, and the last step was to see if we could have that same chemistry and connection in person. *Fast Forward* After our dinner, movie, the beautiful walk in the park, and the piggy back ride. The atmosphere of the whole night was filled with so much laughter and endless conversations, that we ended up having HOT STEAMY SEX. LMAO, LOL, ROTFL, just joking.

I'm a complete jokester. That's my personality and I wanted to give you, the readers a WTF moment. Lol, so please forgive my sense of humor. But back to where I left off. After the endless conversations and laughter it was dark out and we were sitting on the curb in front of her house. We were under the stars and I laid the back of my head in her lap and was thinking to myself that this girl was amazing and she was everything

I want, from her looks to her personality to the mind stimulating conversations. As I walked Mary to the door to conclude the night, I sensed Mary wanted me to kiss her goodnight. But for me, the night was so beautiful and so perfect, that I didn't want to ruin the night by kissing her.

Our chemistry was super strong and after that night I knew I set myself apart from any potential guy that was after her. She was mine to lose. For me that's when *Cuffing Season* began. If she thought I was amazing before just wait until she saw the creative Terry. During my *cuffing season*, I was romantic with her. For example, her favorite R&B group at the time was 'Pretty Ricky' (LOL, yes Pretty Ricky rotfl, remember this is 2004. She was 19 years old.) I purchased the 'Pretty Ricky' CD and put it on her windshield, so when she went to her car she would be surprised. *Side Note* (She lived 75 miles from me one way so you can tell I was feeling her.) Her favorite candy was Almond Joy. So one day I bought a bag of Almond Joys that contained about 200 pieces. I wrapped up the bag in wrapping paper and I wrote a note saying, "Ever since you entered my life you brought me nothing but joy."

Press pause

Keep in mind, Mary and I were just kids during the **cuffing season** and it may seem corny now but being broke kids 19 and 21 years old I had to be creative and as romantic as my funds can take me.

Press Play

Those sweet and romantic things brought the biggest smile to her face. I would write her poetry. I would mail letters to her house every other day to let her know that even though we weren't together physically she was on my mind 24/7. I would drive over an hour one way just to visit her. I would surprise her at her house when she got off work and stay there all night just laughing and talking. I wanted her to know that she was perfect for me, so I bought her a Cinderella slipper and said, "Out of all the women I saw and dated nobody ever made me feel like you. Nobody was a perfect match for me. But when I met you everything about you from your looks to your personality was a perfect match for me. And that's why I'm giving you this slipper, because Mary I swear you are my Cinderella." I wanted to keep her in suspense, so I had a message in a bottle sent to her house. When she received it, the bottle looked like it was washed up on the beach shores just like in the movies. And to keep the suspense, I made it so that she had to pop the cork just to get to the message inside. I dedicated songs to her expressing how I felt. During the *cuffing season* I gave her the best me and I wanted her to know that her hunt for a man was over.

  I wanted her to rest assure that all she would ever want in a man, she had all of that in me. I had a Boost mobile cell phone at the time with free incoming minutes. Mary would call me all the time so the phone calls would be free. We talked for hours at a time and her phone bill ran up super high. She told me about her bill, she was crying and I comforted her by saying "don't worry about the bill I got it." (All the girls I dated in the past can testify that my pockets were super tight and I never spent money on a female like that.) But I took care of the bill because I liked her that much. Nothing else mattered to me. Money didn't matter. The hour drive one way didn't stop me, I just wanted Mary to feel secure and feel security within me.

  I was there for her on all levels and she brought that out in me. She was amazing and I was 100%

sure without a doubt that I wanted her to be mine exclusively. I was nervous to ask her, but the stars aligned perfectly for me. A song played on the radio by Dru Hill called 'I Should Be Your Boyfriend'. I said to Mary during the song, "You know you're my girl right?" she said "Ok." Then I said, "It's official, on the date of September 29th Mary you are officially my girl." And on that date the boyfriend/girlfriend 'relationship handcuffs' were placed on us and we had each other all to ourselves.

Time To Reflect

At this time put the book down and reflect. I mean really get lost in your thoughts and reflect. Reflect on the time before marriage and before you guys were even an official couple.

Husbands: Reflect on the time when you first laid eyes on her. What were the thoughts going through your mind? What did you tell yourself? What made her stand out? What qualities did she possess? What made her different from all the other females? What made you want to enter the *'Cuffing Season?'* What was your *cuffing season* process like? How did you feel inside during the *cuffing season*? What sweet special things did you do for her during the *cuffing season* that set you apart from other dudes? How did you finally put those handcuffs on her and how did you feel when she said yes?

Wives: Reflect on the time when you first laid eyes on him. What did he first say to you and or what was the first conversation like? What made you give him your phone number so that you guys could further communicate? What was the first phone call like? How did you know he was serious about you? What made him stand out from all the other guys? What was the *cuffing season* like through your eyes? How did you feel during the *cuffing season?* What sweet and special things did he do for you and you do for him? What did you do to separate yourself from the other females? How did you feel when he finally put the handcuffs on you?

The Same 3 Course Meal

Appetizer

A preview, a sneak peek, a small taste to keep your interest to entice you, to grow your hunger in anticipation for what is to come.

Cuffing Season was amazing, I just handcuffed my baby and we were official. Life was great. My baby and I were inseparable. We were having fun, building memories with each other, constant smiles on our faces, there was not a problem in the world. We didn't have real jobs and we both lived with our parents, so all that meant to us was that we had no real responsibilities. We had no bills and no stress which also meant that we had more time together. The honeymoon phase of our relationship was so bomb, so good, so fresh and so new that I was eager and excited to see what was next.

    She was everything that I wanted – sexy, beautiful, exotic, smart, funny and witty - that one year into us dating, I gave her a promise ring just to let her know that I was serious. We were going to comedy shows, Vegas, amusement parks, Catalina Island, movies, dinners and we spent lots of quality time with ourselves as well as hanging out together with each other's parents. We cooked together, baked desserts and had sleepovers at her parent's house. Her parents loved me so much that her dad would make me breakfast in the mornings. My boys loved her. They thought she was perfect for me. I can honestly say that this time was the highest point of our freshly new relationship.

About one year and six months into our relationship, we both got career related jobs. I bought my first home in Victorville, California, but it was so far from family and friends, that I decided to rent it out and continue to live rent free with my parents.

We both were making money, living at home with no responsibilities or a care in the world. Life was lovely. Then reality hit us smack in the face. Mary's dad retired from the military and she probably had about three months left in California before relocating back to her hometown of Seattle, Washington. This news ended my world. The future of our relationship relied heavily on our next decision. We talked about having a long distance relationship but we both knew that wasn't going to work. Then we had a brilliant idea that she would just get an apartment in Temecula, California (In the middle of where I was currently residing and she was currently residing) and we could continue our relationship. We looked at apartments. She found one that she liked. I gave her money for the deposit and just like that the problem was solved. We both loved each other, we were at the highest point of our relationship and we would be foolish not to see what was in stored for us next.

  A few days later I thought to myself that I couldn't have my baby living alone in an apartment. I told her my plan. I suggested to her that instead of renting an apartment, we should buy a house together. I figured we both made good money and I was about to buy another house anyway so why not? I also told her that I knew that houses were more expensive than apartments, so I would take care of all the expenses, utilities, groceries, cable, H.O.A fees and all she would pay was the amount she would have paid for the rent somewhere else. To top it off we would both be homeowners and it would be a great investment. She agreed and was so excited. One year and eight months into our relationship we were homeowners. I remember when we got the keys to the house and we slept on the floor together because we had no furniture. Lol, young love at its finest.

  A total of one year and eight months and we were now homeowners. *I'll come back to that in the next section.* But we were beyond happy. I remember coming home from work and as I opened the door, our once bare empty house was completely decorated. My baby turned our house into a home. I would cook for her all the time; my food was so bomb that one day she thought I ordered the food at a restaurant and tried to say I didn't cook it. Lol, I taught her how to cook the foods I grew up on. When we got our house painted we were so excited we were jumping up and down like little kids. We watched TV together, bonded, went on trips, and cuddled. Life was good and we were both eager to see what our lives had in stored for us. The appetizer definitely was amazing and had us wanting more.

Dinner

The most important, and the most nourishing whether positively or negatively depending on what your body is being served. It will grow or cripple you, satisfy or un-satisfy you, and whether you are fulfilled or unfulfilled it is what you will remember the most out of the 3 courses.

Going back to the part where I said I'll come back to that. Well I'm coming back to that. One year and eight months into our freshly new relationship we were homeowners. We went from living at home with no responsibilities to homeowners. We went from not sharing our space, to living together. We went from having our own separate money doing what we wanted, to now budgeting, handling bills, utilities, mortgages, groceries, food, cable, and property taxes. We went from boyfriend and girlfriend to practically being married. S**T just got real in our relationship in a blink of an eye.

The allure, the mystery, the perfection that we both held in each others' eyes was now over. There was no more anticipation and build up of when we would see each other because now we saw each other everyday. No more picking her up at her parent's house and ringing the doorbell and her answering the door looking like an angel from heaven. Because now we are getting dressed side by side in the bathroom. We now had responsibilities and those responsibilities equaled stress which created tension at times. There was no more calling in sick to just chill with each other. I had to work every day because I had grown man bills that needed to be paid. I remember we would go grocery shopping and argue over groceries, about what we needed and what we didn't need.

 She needed a new car and she didn't have the down payment, so I paid it. Reality kicked me in the face and to keep it real, not knowing this at the time, but I began to build up animosities towards Mary. Because instead of me living in the comfort of my parent's house just stacking up money with no responsibilities, I was now penny pinching and living paycheck to paycheck paying bills because Mary had no place to stay. That was what my selfish, self-centered brain was thinking. But in return, what I didn't think about was that Mary sacrificed just as much if not more to be with me. She had no family in California, and if she would have moved with her parents to

Washington she wouldn't have a worry in the world as well.

But she sacrificed all of that to be with me. I didn't see that then, but I sure see that now. I loved her and she loved me but we were so blinded by the sacrifices of love we were making individually, that we didn't see those same love sacrifices being made by the other partner as well. So those sacrifices of love turned into animosity in our hearts towards one another. Well, at least for me it did. The animosity I held in my heart led to an introduction of something new to our relationship which was arguments. Dinner was now being served.

Dessert

"To complete, to conclude and to compliment the nourishing dinner. Or used as an attempt to give a new lasting impression from the unfulfillment of what was being served at dinner."

The newness of our relationship was comparable to the newness of a baby. Our relationship was ready to be molded in any way, shape or form depending on the molder. Our relationship was ready to be taught what was right and what was wrong depending on the teacher. We didn't know it then, but we were both the molder and the teacher and our actions molded and taught our relationship and hearts. One year and eight months together into our new lives, our relationship was like wet cement - it was formed however we wanted it formed, but once the wet cement was formed we only had a little bit of time to reform it before the cement became concrete.

  Our relationship formed into concrete right before our eyes. We loved each other so much but we argued frequently. The love, the passion, and the chemistry we shared overrode the arguments and the foul things said during those arguments. We were young and in love. We gave our arguments the excuse all couples give, which was that all couples fight, all couples argue and that's just what couples do. But as long as we loved each other that's all that mattered. We believed the relationship 'lie' which was that arguing was normal. That was our mind frame and in return that became our new normalcy.

  I loved Mary so much that even during our arguments, my heart always convicted me. My heart always went out to her. When she cried my heart cried. When I hurt her through words my heart hurt. When she felt pain through my words, my heart felt that pain as well. My heart felt everything she felt because I gave her my heart and my heart was so in tuned with hers. We were connected. If we argued, we always apologized. On a scale of 1 to 10 (1 being the lowest and 10 being the highest) was how deep the apology was. So if our argument was a level two, then the apology would be a 3 or a 4 which was just enough to make the other person forget about the argument and focus on the good in us. If the argument was a level six then the apology would be an 8. The level 8 apology would be like "Baby you know you are my heart and I love you so much. I shouldn't have said that or acted like that. I'm so sorry." If the argument was at a level 10, then the apology would be at a level 20. For example, the level 20 apology would be roses, teddy bears, shopping sprees, along with "I'm sorry, I love you", then passionately making up by physical actions. 😍

   We never went to bed mad or angry and we always apologized so the arguments never bled into the next day. We thought we were erasing the arguments through the passionate make up sessions, but we were unknowingly becoming immune to our foul ways. As the arguments continued the "I'm sorry baby" shortly followed but the apologies became less and less meaningful, believable and the apologies started to become routine. After the unfulfillment of dinner and the malnourishment our bodies and hearts were being served, we knew the dessert would be enough to fulfill us. And the dessert on our menus were always the same apologies with the "I love you" on top.

    It was ***the same three course*** meal for us. We would start with the appetizer which was laughing, joking, kissing, hugging, loving, keeping our interest, making us want more of each other. Whether it was the same day, weeks later or a month later, dinner would be served and we would serve each other with arguing which tainted how we felt during the appetizer. The dinner is the most important meal out of the three courses and what we would remember the most. But after each unfulfilled dinner we knew the dessert would come. And we would overcompensate with the dessert and use the dessert as an attempt to make us forget about what we served each other for dinner.

After the dessert, we would go back to the same appetizer, followed by the same dinner and back to the same dessert. It was always *the same three course meal* for us.

Time To Reflect

At this time put down the book and just think about what you just read and think about your relationship. Take yourselves back to the time before the arguing, and what introduced the arguing and verbal fighting

Husbands and Wives: What was the appetizer like in your relationship? What was it that made you want more? Do you remember the first time you served each other with a malnourished dinner? How did you both respond to the malnourished dinner that was served? Were there any built up animosities you may have had towards each other? What was the dessert like? What was the process to make one another forget about what you just served them? Looking back into the past was there anything you could have done to make the dinner nourishing to each other, so that the dessert could have been a compliment to the dinner and not an attempt to make each other forget about the unfulfilling dinner? Is it always *the same 3 course meal* for you two? How would you change it moving forward?

Ride or Die

A loved one you can depend on in a time of need. Loyal, down for you and battle tested. One that can celebrate with you when you are winning and won't abandon you when you are losing. Through thick and thin, whether you are ballin or fallin, they rock with you until the end

🎵 We fly high, no lie, we ballin, BALLIN 🎵 That's how life started to pick up for us. I found a new way to generate more cha-ching-ching from my job which allowed me to bring home $3500 every two weeks which was 7 racks a month in my pocket. Holla!!!! We went from penny pinching to me asking Mary if she wanted me to call in sick and spend quality time with her. And of course Mary's answer was always "Yes". Our 3 course meal was still in effect. But we accepted that. But now life was gravy and even way better than before.

I gave Mary a debit card linked to my account because she was my boo boo and whenever she fell short financially I wanted her to know I had her back. We were eating out constantly and going to movies during the week. I was still winning her heart by showing her the world and being romantic; I was just being the guy she fell in love with. I surprised her with staycations on the Queen Mary, Hollywood, plays, boat rides, and taking her to see her favorite R&B artists Trey Songz, Day 26, Mario, Joe and Chris Brown. I introduced her to new things and new experiences. My baby even took a road trip with me to San Francisco riding shotgun so I can see my boy Ginuwine perform. Money was flowing. Mary showed me what the airplane life was like, flying to various states to see her family, friends, and numerous sightseeing locations. No lie, air mileage was new to me. We had lots of family time. Neither of our parents agreed with us living together before being married, but once they finally accepted it, it allowed us to breathe and relax.

 Mary won my parent's hearts with her personality and bomb cooking. It was good times and easy sailings. But it's easy to pass a test when it's an open book exam. (meaning when life is gravy) But the real test is when the pop quiz comes unexpectedly, how would you do? *Fast Forward a few months* My crew at work had a mishap and we went on a hearing in front of the disciplinary board. We got suspended for six months with no pay. But me being the genius I am, I got a thing called job insurance from my job. So even though I was suspended, I was still making the same amount of money. So the 6 months suspension equaled 6 months vacation time.

So now Mary and I were really enjoying our time together. I'm surprised she didn't end up pregnant 😀 lol. But I was now a heavily paid stay at home boyfriend. She would come home from work and I would have dinner made. I would do projects around the house such as turning the garage into a real room. We cuddled at night, and we really bonded on my time off. Three months into being suspended my co-worker called and explained to me that the job was doing major layoffs due to the economy. He also stated that I was lucky I was suspended because I was the only one who was making consistent pay. To make a long story short, when I got back to work, my job and income wasn't steady and I barely made just enough to survive.

I blew through my savings at this time. Now I'm in a position where choices had to be made. I ended up quitting and I went back to my old measly job. Don't get me wrong, I thank God for the job and no job is measly. I just used that term to let you know that the job didn't pay well at all. I barely made enough to pay the bills. What I promised Mary before we bought the house, I had to break and as a man I hated breaking my promise. With Mary's help financially, we could barely take care of the bills and necessities. Our lifestyle as we knew it was over. No more luxuries, no more shopping sprees, no more restaurants, and no more trips. I kept my financial situation to myself. I had to man up because I refuse to ask for help.

Nobody knew what I was going through but my baby. I felt like a failure. My old coworkers mocked and laughed at me when I got rehired at my old job, but what was way worse than that was as a man I couldn't provide for Mary like I once did. She couldn't get her nails done nor her hair done anymore. It was just the bare necessities. The unexpected pop quiz was here and she passed with flying colors. She was never battle tested in my eyes before this, because there was only an upside being Terry's girl. But on the real, she was getting everything so it was easy to be with me. But now I had hit rock bottom, with nothing to offer her. She was loyal, she rode for me and stood by my side. I was at my worst and she saw the best in me. When I saw a loser she saw a winner. She could have easily packed up and said "Deuces." But she believed in me when I didn't believe in myself, and with her by my side she gave me the reassurance I needed. At that very moment in our lives I realized her worth.

I realized that she was a good woman, and a female with her quality traits were hard to come by. I was blessed to have her. At that moment she was my earth. The earth has its ugliness in it such as smog, war and evilness but it also has beaches, moons, stars, sunsets, and sunrises to make it beautiful. That's why I call her my earth. Because even though our relationship had its ugliness in it such as arguments, I saw the underlining beauty and undeniable love she had for me. During my thunderstorm, she was my sunshine. During my rain, she comforted me by letting me know that after the rain the sun always follows. She was my sunrise when I woke up in the morning, and my sunset when my day ended.

With her being with me when I had nothing to offer her, marrying her was the only thing on my mind. I scraped up my chump change I was making just to get a ring so I can propose to her. I proposed that Christmas of 2008. She said "Yes" and months down the road we got married. As I see her walking down the aisle in a beautiful white dress I realized she loved me unconditionally. As she was walking down the aisle, I was thinking to myself that she was about to trust her life to a bum. She was about to trust her life to a man with a bum job, no money and nothing to offer. As tears ran down my cheek, I said my vows. As she read her vows I realized she loved me in spite of me.

June 27th 2009 I gave her my last name. Through thick and thin from ballin' to fallin', this woman will always be my earth and she earned the title my *Ride or Die*. The love she displayed overrides any arguments. Two months after we said "I Do" and sealed it with a kiss, I got a bomb job making that Cha-Ching-Ching again. Praise the lord. Her loyalty, faithfulness, belief in me and riding for me. She earned the title Mrs. Williams and whatever my wife wanted she got. Whatever her heart desired she got. When I was down and defeated she stayed by my side. She proved her worth and in my book earned my world and everything in it. A famous rapper by the name of Drake once sang 🎵Started from the bottom, now we here. 🎵 When we first met, we had nothing, then one year and eight months later we had everything, then we went back to the bottom, now two houses later and a couple of investments we are here. We literally came up together.

Time To Reflect

Husbands: When did you find out she was your *Ride or Die?* What situation did you go through to let you know she loved you unconditionally, and loved you in spite of yourself? How did you feel knowing her love was real? How did you feel when she proved herself, and her loyalty to you? What made you ask her to be your wife?

Wives: How did you know he was your *Ride or Die?* How did he prove his worth? When you were at your worse how did he let you know he was there for you? How did you know when he truly loved you and was down for you through thick and thin? What made you say "yes" when he asked you to be his wife?

12th Round KnockOut

"When you enter a relationship and ready to go the distance, you know it's going to be a fight to make it. Along the way you are taking blow after blow from your partner and every time you fall from the blows you get back up. Every round the hits are getting harder and the blows are doing more damage. By the 12th round your body, mind, and heart is fatigued and drained. You put up the best fight you can then your partner delivers the final blow that makes you fall. As you are down, you are too tired, too exhausted and your heart finally gives up and the fight is over."

About 2 years after we said "I Do", 2 year after we said our wedding vows and 2 years after our beautiful honeymoon reality was now here and *The Same 3 course meal* was still in effect but the dessert portion was getting smaller and smaller (apologies were not even apologies anymore. It was just a quick sorry to shut the other partner up.) I'm being completely transparent. There was a two week period where I served my wife the most malnourished dinner ever in our life together. And the reason being which is not an excuse, was because I was so caught up in all the sacrifices of love that I was doing, that I failed to see the sacrifices of love that she was doing. My mind had been conditioned that way.

The sacrifices of love quickly became sacrifices to use as ammunition. My pointer finger was my gun and it was filled with the ammunition of "Look what I did. What have you done?" And the gun filled with ammunition was aimed at her. With the gun loaded with ammunition pointing at her, her hands were always held in the air in a surrendering 'don't shoot me stance' as she pleaded "I did this, I did that, why don't you see what I'm doing?" But her pleas were never good enough to me.

Press Pause

Yes I still loved her. Yes I did sweet things. Yes she was my heart. Yes I still spoiled her and yes she was still my earth. But this section isn't for glorification and getting props for what I had done. This section isn't for you the readers to see the best in me. This section is the turning point and how I was being a complete ass, a complete d**k for 2 weeks straight which can cloud every loving act a person does.*

Press Play

Her pleas were never good enough for me. Stupid miniscule stuff would cause an argument like having no bottled waters in the refrigerator. I would take something so small like having no waters in the fridge and then I would make slick underhanded comments to Mary about it. Work being stressful, long hours, the car breaking down and needing a three thousand dollar engine replacement, major stuff breaking down in the house and just dealing with life things were taking a toll on me. And for those 2 weeks Mary was on the receiving end of everything I was dealing with. I created a false perception of Mary which was, ME FEELING UNAPPRECIATED.

When I would do something for her, I would want her reaction to be a certain way and when she didn't give me that reaction I felt hurt. Yeah your boy is a sensitive man lol. But I felt unappreciated and I'm sure she felt unappreciated as well. But for those two weeks our communication was off. Our phone service was disconnected and we had no reception. We both were in Stevie Wonder mode- BLINDED. We were so caught up in what we were doing individually that we didn't see what the other person was doing. I'm the man so I'm going to take the blame. If I would have opened my eyes and saw her sacrifices of love, I would have realized we were on the same team. For those two weeks I was being a complete d**k, a complete ass because I felt the weight of the world on my shoulders.

The Turning Point Mary was supposed to wake me up for work at 9pm. She got home from work at 6pm. She was super exhausted from working all day that when she got home, she was so drained she fell asleep. Well you already know what happened next. She didn't wake me up. I was fed up. To me this was the last straw. I was blinded by the fact that she was exhausted from work. The only thing I saw was unappreciation and that she didn't have my back. I told her she was selfish and didn't look out for me. And after going on and on for about 5 minutes, I then said the unthinkable. "Let's not be together anymore. I can't deal with this anymore."

She was hurt and devastated. No apologies came out of my mouth after that was said. The next two days was distant between us. Then a week later we were laying next to each other in bed and she asked did I mean those words. I said, "No, I was just mad." Then I noticed she wasn't being the same forgiving Mary. We were talking but the atmosphere was cold and something was super off. That night we talked. She said, "Why are we even together? You don't appreciate me. You truly hurt me to the core and I knew you meant those words you said about 'It's Over'. (at this time every good, loving, supporting thing I had done was out the window. Because the bad actions always outweigh the good.)

  I rebutted by saying "You don't appreciate me. You take me for granted." She replied by saying, "I take her for granted." That conversation quickly turned into an argument. Then she said, "I don't deserve to be treated like this." I told her the exact same words because I was clouded as well. Then she said those words that killed my heart and were unforgivable. She said "YOU DONT TREAT ME WELL! NO MAN WOULD EVER TREAT ME LIKE YOU AND I KNOW I CAN DO BETTER."

  My heart instantly broke. In my head I was saying WTF. Out of all the things I had done. Then I said, "I feel the exact same way you do and I bet a lot of women would appreciate the things I do, the hard work I do and would love all of my good qualities unlike you. I KNOW I CAN

DO BETTER TOO." And just like that those two weeks of mistreatment and those hurtful words hardened our hearts. Those words overrode years of us being together and just like that our marriage was over. The knockout blow was delivered on both of our ends. We both were too drained and too exhausted to fight anymore, and our hearts gave up.

Time To Reflect

Put down the book, and just reflect on your relationship. Reflect only on the hardest time of your relationship

Husbands: What was your *12th round knockout* blow like? How did you feel? How long were you fighting before your heart gave up? Could you have gotten back up from the knockout blow? Did you deserve the knockout?

Wives: What was your *12th round knockout* blow like? How long were you in the fight for? How did your heart break? What was the final blow that made you fall? How tired were you?

The Mirror Doesn't Lie

"When you visualize yourself in a certain way in your head, and the false facade you see yourself in becomes YOUR TRUTH. But when you look in the mirror, the way you visualize yourself and the reflection in the mirror are the complete opposite. When you are looking at your reflection you don't even recognize the person you are looking at in the mirror. That's when you realize the facade you saw yourself in is a lie, and the truth is staring right back at you in the mirror.*

I can't speak for Mary, but my heart was super drained, and it had given up. In my mind and heart my marriage was OVER. That night we slept in different rooms. The next day Mary was ready to forgive me, wanted me to forgive her and to just move on from this bad situation. She was apologetic, was very emotional and said she didn't mean anything she said. She told me I was everything she ever dreamt of in a man and nobody could ever compare to me. She also said that I was being very mean to her, snapping on her, being insensitive to her and that's why she said those cruel things to me.

Then she said that she isn't going to let those two weeks of mean actions by me define the man I am and define how I have loved her, cared for her and provided for her.

   But me on the other hand, my heart was already cold and my mind was made up. I completely ignored every word in that apology she said. I had a blank stare on my face and that's when she realized she was talking to a brick wall and this fight was more serious than she thought. I was at a tug of war with myself. It was seriously like the cartoons; the devil was on my left shoulder and the angel was on my right shoulder both sounding very convincing in my ear. The devil was saying, "How dare she say that B.S. to you, talking about she could do better. Can you believe that? She said she can do better after all the things you have done." Then the angel replied in my ear saying, "She only said that because you were being very mean and insensitive and to Mary's defense, you said it to her first, when she didn't wake you up for work." The devil then cuts off the angel and says, "Come on Terry. Where's your manhood at? She straight said she is done with you." The angel cuts off the devil and says, "But Terry you said you were done with her first, how else is a woman supposed to feel after hearing that?" The devil and angel start arguing back and forth about who was right and who was wrong and that's when I acted just like the cartoons and I flicked the angel off of my shoulder and sided with the devil. "IT'S OVER!!!!" I said with authority as I slammed the door shut.

I called in sick that night because I was in no position to work.

As I laid in bed, tossing and turning I could not sleep because I was visualizing life after Mary. I visualized Mary dating a new guy and replacing me. My mind was running wild. You know the part of the book when I write about *The Dream and The Nightmare*, well what I was visualizing as I laid in my bed was the Nightmare section times 1,000 and on steroids on top of that. It was the worst nightmare ever because one day that nightmare would become reality since we are no longer together. I shook off the nightmarish thoughts and I visualized me as a bachelor getting back into the dating world. I am very religious, I am a Christian and I believe in God. I am in no way, shape or form trying to preach to anyone. But God gave me the realist revelation ever that I so much needed.

As I looked into the mirror the revelation hit my heart hard. I looked at my reflection in the mirror and I really didn't recognize who I was looking at. Then as I continued to look I saw that the unrecognizable person was me. As I looked in the mirror I saw how ugly I had become. I saw the ugliness in me, I saw the anger in me. I saw my nasty ways and actions towards my wife. I saw the slick remarks, short tempers and I saw every single ugly trait I had. I didn't even recognize the man I become.

As I slept that night my heart literally went super in depth about my ugliness. It may be 'JUST' a sentence to you the reader but for me that night of revealing my ugliness lasted for an eternity.

The next day I walked in the bathroom in the master bedroom and stared at the mirror. Mary came in. I swear I'm being very transparent right now. I looked Mary in the eyes, and as my eyes were filled with tears I said, "Mary I'm sorry. Mary I AM SORRY. You are my wife and I shouldn't have ever treated you like that. I'm very sorry. I'm supposed to protect you, build you up, but in return I destroyed you with my words and broke you down." As tears flowed down my face and my heart was being emptied I said, "I apologize for every argument I caused, every fight I caused and every disrespectful word I have said knowingly and unknowingly. I am sorry for every time I hurt you. I am sorry." Mary started to cry and she began to say her apologies and my heart was emptied from the animosities I ever held. My heart was emptied from my ugly ways because honestly that was the first time in a looong time I apologized and meant every word of it. And Mary felt it during my apologies. Yeah I apologized in the past but it was a "yeah, yeah, I'm sorry whatever, let's just move on." But this one I actually meant.

I owned my actions and took accountability for my ugliness towards Mary and from the bottom of my heart I apologized and actually meant my apology. My heart was emptied from the burdens, emptied from the animosities and strife I held as well. And it felt like a ton of bricks was lifted off of my heart.

****Time To Reflect****

"As you just finished reading the 'Mirror Doesn't Lie' put yourself in this section and really reflect and ask yourself these questions;*

Husbands: What is the image you have of yourself? Does the image you see yourself in and the reflection in the mirror match? Think about how ugly you been? Think about how your ugliness effects the relationship? Have you ever really apologized for your ugly actions and meant every word? As you think about your ugly actions are you happy or ashamed of the man you become? You should really have a talk with your wife about your ugliness!!!

Wives: What is the image you have of yourself? Does the reflection in the mirror match how you see yourself? Think about how ugly you been? Why were you so ugly? How did your ugly actions affect the relationship? Have you ever apologized for your ugly ways and meant every word of the apology? Is your ugly ways the real you? Who is the real you? Are you happy or ashamed of the person have you become?
You should really have a one on one conversation with your husband about your ugliness!!!

The New Twin Towers

"When you have been broken, crushed, defeated and lost with no belief and confidence in yourself. The same defeat, the same broken-ness, the same life obstacle that destroyed you, are the same memories that rebuilds you. Through the smoke, the dust, the rubble, and the remembrance of the Twin Towers, you realize the greatness, the significance, the worth and you rebuild the New Twin Towers. Stronger, better, newer and the New Twin Towers have more meaning now than it ever did because of the rise, the fall and the rebuild it went through. *

I know what you guys are thinking, "Ok cool he apologized. It was really heartfelt and Mary can tell he meant every last word. Now they resumed their marriage and lived happily ever after." NO, NO, NO to the HELL NO! It was not that easy in my head and in my heart. In my brain and in my heart, I apologized for being ugly because nobody deserves that treatment, especially my wife. I needed to apologize and really empty my heart of all its animosities and its ugliness. Because my wife deserved and needed to hear that genuinely. And as a man I needed to finally own it, admit my faults, take ownership of it and let her know that I saw what she lived through during that two week period. But even after pouring out my heart to Mary, the marriage was still completely over. My confidence was broken. I felt betrayed when she said those treacherous words to me. To hear those words, "I don't deserve her and she knows she can be treated better by someone else" crushed my heart and shattered my confidence. But if it wasn't for those life shattering words then I would not have had the self-revelation. On the flipside those words crippled me, killed me, and I didn't think I could come back from that. My wife is supposed to feel protected and feel her husband is her protector. My wife is supposed to think I was the 'end all be all' when it comes to men. My wife is supposed to feel she hit the lottery when she found me. She is supposed to feel that no other man could even fill my shoes nor even compare to me.

   When she released those bombshells from her mouth and it hit me, it made me collapse. Crushed, defeated, lost and weakened was the feeling I had as I laid in my bed that night. As I was laying down God did something so amazing and showed me something that I really needed to see. The day before he revealed the type of person I had become. Tonight he revealed to me, THE REAL ME. The pure me, the unclouded me. God revealed to me how beautiful I was. Not on the outside but the inside. The inner beauty overrides the outer. God showed me my inner beauty and showed me how one of a kind and unique I was. He uncovered memories of myself that were covered by the drama, bills, stress, work, arguments, animosities and just life. And after I was completely uncovered, my eyes were open, what was cloudy was now finally clear. God gave me visions, gave me beautiful images of myself, like how Mary and I first met. He showed me the constant smiles and joy I always had on my face and on her face as well. He showed me my one of a kind beautiful personality.

As I laid in my bed my heart was getting filled with love, happiness and understanding. Thoughts of the past shined like the sunshine does through the clouds. Thoughts and the beauty of our first phone conversation of how we laughed, joked, and had deep talks entered my mind. Followed by hearing her smiling through the phone, and the joy I constantly brought to her. Then I was revealed how much chemistry we had, how much passion we shared for one another, how romantic, how sweet, how caring, how sensitive, how comforting, and how selfless I was. I remembered a lot of beautiful things but the memory that rebuilt me completely was God showing and revealing to me that I was the person she fell in love with, I was the person that made her feel so loved, and even when I lost everything she still married me because I WAS 'THE END ALL BE ALL' MAN TO HER. And she loved me because I was so beautiful to her in every way. That's when I realized those destructive words she said were a complete lie and totally false. Because of my beautiful revelation, beautiful memories, beautiful thoughts of how I was and how I could be beautiful in the future, I became restored. I was made whole, my heart was filled with new blood, and at that moment, I was more confident in myself than I ever was before because now I was self-aware.

****Time to Reflect****

Put yourself in those shoes. My story may be different from yours, but the point of the story is still the same.

Close your eyes and think about **'The New Twin Towers'** *in you**

Husbands and Wives: If you are down and defeated at this moment, what could you do to rebuild yourself? Think about how beautiful you are as a person on the inside? Don't think about yourself at this current state but think about how you both fell in love with each other and fell in love with the qualities you both possess. You are still the person your partner fell in love with but somehow you both lost your way. Think about how you lost your way? Once you see how you lost your way, you are now found. Use those beautiful memories to help rebuild yourself and to make yourself stronger and have more confidence.

Real Talk

"When you have the most honest, the most serious, and the most heart to heart conversation with your partner you ever had. During the talk, the conversation is not sugar coated, nor is the conversation to protect a person's feelings. It's the most rawest, the most uncut, the most realest conversation you will have with someone to get your point across to make a drastic change."

My mind and heart were completely restored. I was once broken but now I was rebuilt stronger than ever. I was full of new confidence, full of new self-awareness within myself that I needed to have the most realest conversation with Mary. The conversation I would have with Mary would be the most serious conversation we ever had in our lives together. As soon as I sat Mary down to have a conversation she snapped on me and said with an argumentative tone, "Let's move on from this, it's not that serious." I sat calm and once she was finished I said with a stern tone, "I am tired of this arguing, fighting and not knowing how to talk to each other. Do I want to be back with you? I honestly don't know. But if we are going to be like the old us then the answer is no. We both don't deserve that. If I can't give you my all and vice versa we don't need to be together."

  I also told her about what was revealed to me. I explained how I was extremely broken and defeated by the 'I Can Do Better' words she said to me. I also told her about the revelation I had which was me seeing the beautiful me. I also explained how the revelation restored me and gave me a whole new outlook on everything. I told her that there is life after us. I am a beautiful person and she is a beautiful person as well and we both have extremely great qualities and quality traits someone would love. I further explained that if we decide to make it work all we can do is give our all and if it doesn't work out we don't need to be sad because what we don't love, appreciate or cherish about each other, someone else will. There is someone out there that would love to enjoy us and what we have to offer. I then told her that I'm through arguing and this is the most critical and most crucial point of our marriage because nothing is keeping us here.

  We have no kids, no real ties to each other so this decision really needed to be thought out. I was going to do what I felt was best for me and she had to do what's best for her. I told her I loved her with all my heart but I honestly didn't know if I wanted this anymore.

I'm very excited I went through the whole breaking down and rebuilding process of myself because I needed to see the ugliness in order to see my beauty. Now that I found the beauty in me, I will never lose my beauty again. I was lost but now I'm found and it is a beautiful thing. If this marriage ended I learned a valuable lesson. Always be the best me no matter what. Always be the beautiful me and never let anyone allow me to lose who I am as a person.

I am far from a hater so I uplifted Mary as well. I told her she is extremely beautiful on the inside and out. I told her she has bomb qualities that any man would fall in love with, respect and cherish, and that she doesn't need to be sad if our marriage doesn't work because there is life after me. Maybe even a better life after me. She tried to hug and kiss me and say she only wanted me. But I told her that I couldn't hug or kiss her because my heart was not there. My heart was not in it and I refuse to be fake. She knew I was serious by my actions, words, and the look on my face. I was dead serious and I refused to live my life happy one moment, unhappy the next. The rollercoaster ride was over in my life and whether she accepted it or not she knew the ride was over as well. We both knew in our hearts that our journey, our marriage together could really be over.

  We loved each other so much but it just wasn't clicking for us, and at that moment I told her what both of us knew needed to be said. We were just so caught up in the stagnant, complacent living that we thought that life was supposed to be like that. Before ending the conversation, I reiterated that there is life after us, then I told her I cut off the internet, television and phones because we really needed to think about either continuing or ending our marriage. Because right now I didn't know if I want to stay married or not. As Mary was sitting in her room with no distractions, no tv, no internet and with no phone. I told her to really think about *The Real Talk*, we just had to determine what we really wanted.

Time To Reflect

This section, this last chapter is very self explanatory. As you read 'The Real Talk' I had, Think about yourself and your marriage and what needs to be done.

Husbands and Wives: Maybe it's that time to have a 'Real Talk' conversation with your spouse, and during the 'Real Talk' session be 100% transparent. Talk about the issues you see that is causing you to have that 50/50 feeling of staying or leaving. Really talk to each other and tell your spouse the importance, significance and the severity of the conversation. If it is something your spouse is doing wrong or something you don't like, or even if it's something you dislike about the direction of the marriage, now is the time to express your feelings, thoughts, solutions and conclusions during the 'Real Talk' conversation.

Trust the Process

"When you develop a fail proof plan and you believe and have 100% faith in that plan. You follow the plan's path being completely un-bias, accepting whatever it is at the end of the path. Whatever you discover at the end of the path is the answer to what your heart seeks."

    For three straight days it was cold in my household. I was at home but I barely had any contact with Mary. No eye contact, no communication, not even a "Hi". I cut off all contact purposely because I didn't want to get swayed in any direction. I wanted my decision to be what I really and truly wanted and what was best for me. That's why for three straight days I was drowned in my own thoughts. I came with the 'keep to myself and shut off the world' plan to get the answers I sought. I believed in my plan and I trusted the process I was going through. I purposely did not communicate with the world. I was M.I.A and nowhere to be found. I was on the back of the milk carton 'have you seen him if so contact your local authorities type of missing.' But I was very alive in my own thoughts and that was my plan.

When I'm alone I like to express myself through writing, whether poetically, lyrically or in letter form. So during this intense process, something compelled me to get a notebook and start writing. For three straight days I wrote down every thought and emotion, I was feeling at that exact time. I wrote about how Mary and I met, our beautiful past, how I did things different with her than any other female I ever dated. I wrote about how I took my time to get to know her rather than just trying to hook up with her. I wrote about the strong foundation our relationship was built on, wrote about the good times, our laughs, jokes, vacations we took, talked about our chemistry, passion, fire and desire we had for each other.

  I wrote about our first date, the perfection, and the beauty I saw in her. I reminisced with the pen about asking her to be my girlfriend and how she proved her worth when I lost everything and felt worthless as a man and she still stood by my side. I wrote about the wedding day and how she walked down the aisle towards me. The notebook was my therapy, it was my counselor, it was my ear to listen and as I wrote, I did not only mention the good times, I mentioned the bad times as well. I wrote about our arguments, our fights, and how that made me feel. I wrote about our complacency, our lackadaisical ways, our selfish ways, our unappreciative ways and how it took a toll on our marriage. I wrote about my ugliness and finally apologizing from the heart. I wrote about my beauty and how I rediscovered myself, and I just dwelled on that subject. I wrote about how it would feel to give my all to a new woman, and have a fresh start with a fresh new beginning.

  I wrote about how a woman would fall head over heels for the new beautiful me and I would be exactly what the new girl desired and wanted. I compared my current situation and the lack of appreciation I was getting to how a new female that experienced heartbreak before would love me in her life. As well as appreciate everything I would bring to the table. I also wrote about having *Cuffing Season* with a new female, being in the honeymoon phase with her and never coming out of the honeymoon phase. Because now I know it is very important to never lose my beautiful self and always be the best me. I wrote about winning another girl's heart. I just wrote whatever came to my mind. And I concluded my writing of my thoughts with no biasness, I concluded with no swaying of the heart and I concluded by writing about how NO OTHER FEMALE WILL EVER have my heart the way Mary does. No other female will ever capture my interest and attention the way Mary does.

  My brain, body, soul and heart was all for Mary. Yes, the hunt sounded interesting and getting 'gassed up' by other females would be flattering. But in my eyes I wanted my wife. Through thick and thin I wanted Mary back. I had been there and done that with other females. I married Mary for a reason. Through my writings, the good, the bad and the ugly, my heart answered all the questions I had, which helped me see that without a doubt I wanted Mary. I loved her more than life itself. And now with my revelation of my new rediscovered self I wanted to give Mary my 100%.

  I wanted to love Mary like I never loved anyone before. The old Terry loved Mary more than words can describe, but now I wanted the new Terry to love Mary way more than I previously did. I wanted to be that man she once fell in love with but on a higher scale. I also wrote about how there is no point in searching for another female when everything I truly wanted, desired and loved, I already had in Mary. I wrote about my ultimate fantasy with Mary and no not a sexual fantasy. But a fantasy of being deeply in love with each other, having fun, and being young in love like we once were even though we had adult responsibilities. I also wrote about my ultimate fantasy of combining our deep love we have for one another and creating babies.

I also wrote about my personal promise to her which was to never be complacent and always stay in *'Cuffing Season'*. I vowed to always put her first and always be in the winning her heart mode. And once I won her heart, I would start over and win it again and again and again. My writings became so therapeutic to me and I needed that. I needed to release my thoughts. My mind was now 100% clear. My heart, mind, body and soul were all on the same page. I wanted Mary back. I trusted the process and I had clarity of what I wanted. That night I went to work. I texted Mary to look under her bed. I also texted her that I had something for her to read and after reading it to just text me back either YES or NO.

Time to Reflect

Husbands and Wives: What would be your process? Are you willing to trust your process? Are you willing to accept the answers you have been seeking during the process? What is your ultimate goal? What changes are willing to make? What does your heart truly want? Everybody's process is different. I trusted the process, followed it and gained clarity throughout that time.

The Rebirth

When you survive death and now see things completely different. You now appreciate life, you take nothing for granted and you actually stop and smell the roses. When you make a conscious decision to change permanently. Saying bye to the old you and hello to the new you. When you right your wrongdoings. When you failed the first time and have been given a second chance.

The last page of the 55 page notebook consisted of letting her know that she was my world and despite anything and everything we faced I loved her more than that. My love for her erased any flaw and any bad thing she had done or said to me. I wrote that there was no need to search for another woman because I truly had everything in her. I also let her know that if she does agree to take me back that she would have 100% of me. She would have the new and improved me. She would have the new found me. I'm far from a hater so I also wrote in the notebook and let Mary know there is life after me as well. That she is a beautiful person on the inside and out and a man would love to have a woman like her by their side. I told her she is loyal, trustworthy, a 'ride or die' woman with a great personality. I told her she can start off fresh and have a new start with someone else.

I painted a beautiful picture for Mary. I wanted her to understand that I'm not the end of the world. And I did that because I want her answer to be genuine and not swayed by me. I wanted her to see all sides, so the answer she would give me would be a honest one from the heart and what she truly wanted.

At 8:30pm I gave her the 55 page notebook and I gave her instructions to either respond with a 'YES or NO' text. It was now 4am I was finally on my lunch break. I was super nervous. As I turned on my phone, what usually took 30 seconds to turn on felt like an hour to turn on. As soon as my phone turned on, my phone decided to reboot and upgrade itself. OMG! I thought as I waited for an eternity as I watched from the turtle's point of view as he raced the hare. You know the famous race, the turtle vs the hare and how the turtle moved extremely slow. That's how it was watching the phone reboot. The percentage to completion was going slower and slower, moving from 0% to 3%, then 3% to 7%. Five minutes literally went by and the percentage to completion was only at 30%.

My heart was racing and I thought to myself what if the answer is 'NO'? Well my phone finally reboots and the text messages of text messages came in. I opened her message and it read 'NO'. I dropped my expensive phone shattering it on the ground, I then dropped to my knees and screamed "Nooooooooooo." LOL ROTFL HAHAHAHHAHAAHAAAA. In reality, I opened the message and it read 'YES.' The biggest smile appeared on my face. An adrenaline rush came through my body and I felt so relieved so happy and so rejuvenated getting that 'YES' response. On the way home from work at 6:30am, I called Mary, and we just talked and talked. Keep in mind we hadn't talked, communicated, or even had eye contact for three days during the process.

We talked and she expressed how she felt about my 55 page notebook filled with my thoughts. She told me she cried and was so nervous the whole way through. She apologized for all the actions and ugliness she showed me. She expressed to me that she cried at the end after reading that I wanted to be with her and only her. She was emotional during the 55 page roller coaster of emotions because she didn't know where my heart was.

I explained to her that every loop, turn, twist, that the roller coaster took her on was my transparent honest to God feelings at that time. I told her I was not going to give the notebook to her originally because I was just using the writings as a form of healing and therapy. But when I made up my mind to be with her I felt I needed her to read every emotion I had so she could see my state of mind and how I was 100% sure I wanted her without a doubt. I told her I went from being done with her and ready to move on to being more in love with her than I ever had before. And that right there proves that my unconditional love I had for her was real. We talked about the past on my commute home.

When I was almost home I said to her, "Yes we had a beautiful past, but our past is not going to keep us together. We have to use the past as a learning tool so history doesn't repeat itself." When I pulled into the driveway I realized I would never forget how important this day was to me. I said to her, "Baby I haven't seen you nor have I spoken to you in three days. I don't know what to expect when I come through those doors."

We hung up the phone. I opened the door and she was coming down the stairs. To the naked eye, she was just wearing pajamas with her hair messy because she was fresh out of bed. But to me when I saw her, I saw the most beautiful woman in the world and it felt like I saw her for the first time.

When she came to me I hugged her so tight and as I hugged her I picked her up, then I put her back down still hugging her. As we were still wrapped in each others arms, my heart just spoke and I said, "Baby I love you. Baby you are my world, my heart and my heartbeat. I'm sorry for the things I said and for my ugly ways. But baby even then from the bottom of my heart I still loved you. But even though I loved you then, that love I had for you is over. I don't want to ever love you like that again. I want to love you better, stronger, and my love will continue to grow for you the remainder of my life on this earth. I want my actions to show that I love you. I have no animosities towards you. I will always be the best me for you and I promise every day until I take my last final breath, I will show you the best me. You are my wife, my world and you are the missing piece to my puzzle which completes me."

As we hugged, I could tell that my heart and her heart needed that hug. Our hearts felt like they were at peace again. And those words I told her came from the bottom of my heart. After we hugged I said, "Baby wow! That was the first time in a very long time I hugged you and actually meant it. Yeah I hugged and kissed you before, but it was always a quick hug and peck on the lips. But this I truly meant." I then told her that's why I didn't want to hug her before my mind was made up. Because if I would of hugged her while I was still unsure if I wanted to be with her or not then the hug would have been a nonchalant hug. I then told her that everything from here on out will be done with purpose because it would mean that much more.

****Time to Reflect****

As you read this chapter, put yourself in our shoes. Think and fantasize how the rebirth will be between you and your partner

Husbands and Wives: How would your **rebirth** go? What would be said? How would you express yourself? Would you be 100% transparent? When was the last time you both hugged each other and really meant it? Do you miss each other? Do you honestly want the relationship to move forward? Do you forgive each other of any wrong doings that brought you both to this point? Do you think you both can learn from the past and not make the same mistakes in the future?

I'm Back

*When you feel reborn, refreshed, and rejuvenated. A term you use when you have been gone and away for so long that you suddenly surprise the person that has been missing you. And when they finally see you again, you use that phrase **'I'm Back'**. When a person says **'I'm Back'** that's a definitive meaning that they aren't going anywhere.*

After the long overdue heartfelt hug, we just sat on the couch and just conversed with one another. We were on a natural high. The feeling was euphoric. After just sitting and enjoying each others company, Mary had to get dressed to attend a birthday party and I was going to go to dreamland after getting off of work. I told Mary before I went to sleep to not wake me up and to not tell me bye when she leaves the house. I also said to her, "I want you to look super nice, dress up and look like a runway model like you usually do, because when you are done with the birthday party and you come home I want to see how sexy and beautiful you look."

Three hours later Mary texted me that she was on her way home. I purposely ignored the text. She pulled up to the house looking for me. My car was gone and the house was empty. She called me, but I ignored the call, because my well thought out, executed plan was already in motion. Mary was all alone in the dark house, puzzled as to where I could be. As she was walking, she saw something that looked odd and out of place. She walked over to the out of place object and there it was laying in the middle of the floor in the living room. It was a note. Mary picked up the note clueless and it read,

> Hey baby bear,
> don't text me, don't call me.
> Just meet me at the address below
> 12345 dreamland way
> Temecula, ca, 92562
> See you soon MI Amor.

I'm already at the address waiting patiently, and nervously. As I waited for my beautiful wife to arrive I start going over my game plan in my head. Fifteen minutes later I see Mary's car zooming down the street. To the naked eye it looked like she was running from the cops after robbing a bank. I could have sworn she ran a red light. But I see Mary driving up to the location and giving herself a one last look over in the mirror. I say to myself, "That's my girl." lol.

  She finally pulls up next to me and we lock eyes and I looked her up and down and said to her, "You see now why I didn't want to see you before you left the house? Because if I had I would have been half asleep and I wouldn't have appreciated all of this beauty in front of me." She laughed. Then I held her hand and I said, "Baby let's just get some pizzas and just watch a movie tonight." she said, "OK." I held her hand and walked towards the 'Little Caesars'. I took three more steps in that direction and said, "Nah, I'm just kidding." Rotfl, we both laughed. I said, "Do you trust me?" She said, "yes." I then blindfolded her and put her in the passenger seat of my car. Before I started the car I said, "Baby I made a special music playlist for us, so as the music plays just listen to the words I speak to you. So just sit back and enjoy the ride."

  As I drove I just talked about the music I chose and the significance it has to me and how I felt at that exact moment. I talked about life, my relationship goals, love, and what she means to me. We finally pull up to the destination, I get her out of the car with her back facing the sign so she wouldn't see where we were. I then I took off the blindfold, and when her eyes opened there I was in front of her looking so fly, so smooth, dressed to impress, looking debonair and scrumptious. Lol, rotfl but on the real I was looking pretty fresh, but there I was as the blindfold was removed and she saw my big ass smile on my face holding one dozen roses. She gave me a big hug then I turned her around and her mouth dropped. She responded by saying, "Oh my God." I then said, "baby, here we are, this is our first date I ever took you too. Claim Jumpers, our very first dinner together."

We had an amazing dinner. We talked, laughed, joked, reminisced and had real conversations. I told her I wanted to take her to Claim Jumpers so we could rewind time to the young and innocent us. I told her that we must learn from the past, grow, evolve but as we evolve we can still be young in love. Then out of nowhere Mary said she had something for me. She handed me a card with sweet words in it. At that moment I knew we were both self-aware of what could have happened between us, and with that scary thought it allowed us to be rebirthed, appreciative, and back in the honeymoon phase. We both had the look in our eyes that we will be honeymooning from now until our last breath on this earth. It felt good seeing her on the same page as me as I read her card.

As dinner ended we paid for our meal. I got up first and extended my hand to hers so she could get up next. As she was getting up she jerked back into her seat. I said, "Baby what's wrong?" She explained that she was stuck in the booth we were sitting in. We looked closer and her purse had somehow got caught into the crack of the booth and got stuck, preventing her from getting up. We both laughed and I said, "Only you Mary, only you. But you know I love your clumsy ass. I love everything about you." We finally headed home and on the drive back Mary said, "It felt good. It felt like we were kids again with you leaving me a scavenger note on the floor to meet you at a secret location and being blindfolded to the destination. It felt exciting."

When she said that it felt good, I felt rejuvenated, restored, reborn and I realized this is me. This is who I am. I love being suspenseful, romantic, and full of surprises. I love the hunt for

Mary's heart and love, and I told myself "Terry is Back and will always remain in *Cuffing Season'* winning her heart over and over again and making her fall in love with me over and over again." I told myself I would never stop. In the past I stopped but now I learned from my mistakes. I saw the ugly and my beauty was revealed. Now I got a second chance with the love of my life and I will never stop being the beautiful person I am. I am officially back and here to stay.

****Time to Reflect****

* As you finish reading, put the book down for a moment. Think about the future. Don't think about your current situation in your relationship but fantasize about the future and how you want things to be with your spouse. *

Husbands and Wives: If you were given a second chance with your spouse how would you change things? What is your version of *'I'm Back'*?

And what would it be like? How good would you both feel to be officially back? You control your destiny, your mind and your actions no matter how your spouse acts, you can always stay in the *'I'm Back'* phase without regressing.

Fasting

When you restrain from something you like to do or you give up a specific thing that's important to you. When you sacrifice something you do routinely and you cut it off and stop doing it for a certain period of time to build a stronger connection, relationship and bond with your partner.

Going back to the very first spot where it all began was amazing and symbolic for us. Now we were at home. Emotions were high, the yearn for each others touch was present. So you already know what happens next? Or do you? Bwahahahahaha (evil genius laugh) Well we were kissing passionately, and the way we kissed felt like I hadn't kissed her lips in years. Intimacy and passion were definitely in the air. Me being the man I am, and me leading my household, I said to her, "Baby we can't do this." She asked, "why? I need you." (yes, I am very irresistible. j/k) But on the real she said, "Why?" I said in the voice of Jephte from the tv show 'Married at first sight', "Baaaaaaaby steps." It was an inside joke we both shared and we both died laughing. But I explained to her about how our bond was so deep and so strong when we first met back in the day and I wanted to get that back again. I explained to her that right now we were just super happy we have a second chance with each other and that right now we are just high off of emotion. I said to her, "We are married. Sex and lovemaking will always be there, but baby just trust in me, trust my process on this subject and I got us."

We continued to kiss and hug passionately and I decided to give her one of the best things she liked, which was a massage. After the massage we laid in bed and just talked. We literally talked from 10pm until 3am. We talked about everything from deep conversations to silly convo between us. Then it hit me. I said, "Baby do you see now?" She was clueless. I explained to her what I meant. I said, "You see how we are being intimate right now by just talking and bonding? What if we would have been physically intimate. We would have been sleep right now. But we held off and we connected mentally through conversation."

Honestly it felt like it was the first time we talked in a long time. Don't get me wrong, we always talked. But the talk was a whatever talk, complacent, nonchalant talk. The difference with this talk was that I actually enjoyed the conversation and was engaged in it. I made up my mind to sacrifice our sexual needs for the betterment and growth of our marriage. I gave up sex so we could really get to know, learn and study each other again without the cloudiness of sex. As the days went by I left letters under her pillow at night to read. After she would get off of work I would have dinner made and her bath water ready. There were days where Mary would have my favorite meals prepared surprising me with the things I like.

We would talk on the phone excitingly to and from work. I would give her random massages just because I wanted to and I knew that's what she liked. See I learned from the past and back then I would tend to do sweet gestures so I could get physically intimate. I would be extra nice or give her a massage because the carrot that is dangling in front of me and motivating me to do those nice things was sex. With sex being obsolete we were both catering to each other's needs because we wanted to. We attended to each other, were super nice, patient, loving, sensitive and sweet to each other because of the love we have towards one another. There was no motive to be nice and loving. We did those things because now we were putting each other first.

With sex out of the picture we rediscovered each other. I was loving every bit of it. We kissed passionately when we saw each other and hugged each other tight not wanting to let go. Our bond, chemistry, and passion was going through the roof during this process.

I would leave 'Good Morning' sticky notes on her car steering wheel so she could see it in the morning. I would pop up at her job for surprise lunch dates. I would plan unexpected staycations for us. And on the 19th of the month I wanted to make Mary feel super special. It wasn't our anniversary or birthday or anything special. But to me the nineteenth would always be a special date to me and hold a special place in my heart. The reason being is because the nineteenth was the day I walked through the doors of my house and Mary and I decided to give love and our marriage a second chance.

The 19th was just a regular day for Mary. She came home from work like normal. I told her to go to the guest bedroom. Of course, I blindfolded her. (I guess I do like blindfolds huh?) I did not want her to see what I had planned or have the surprise spoiled. When she walked in the room, I had slow jams playing. I laid her on the bed and gave her the best massage ever. Massaging her with special oils and rubbing her feet to let her know that I was aware she had a long day at work. As I was massaging her, I talked to her and told her how special this day was for me. And I explained that the nineteenth marks one month of the new and improved us, the new and improved love we share, and the new and improved way we do things.

The 19th marks one month of us loving each other the way we both deserved. I told her to remove the blindfold and she was amazed when she saw the dark room only being lit by candles. Then she saw a single rose with a card and cockily I said, "You aren't ready for the new Terry. I'm back baby."

Three months went by of the no sex process. And our relationship and marriage took off to new heights. We were being more intimate and more passionate. When we kissed, WE KIIIIIISED. There were no more cheap hugs and kisses. We would make love to each other mentally and emotionally. One day we were talking on the phone and she said that she feels that she got her best friend back in me. My process worked because now we had rediscovered each other, were more passionate, we're not taking each other for granted, we were doing things from the heart, we were bonding in all ways and in return we became lovers and best friends again.

Now when I look at Mary, I'm seeing her with new eyes and loving her with a new heart. The new foundation was built now we can bond physically. WOOT WOOT!!!!

Time To Reflect*

*After reading the '*Fasting*' chapter what are you guys thinking? Do you want to have the relationship and bonding you had with your spouse in the very beginning, but have it newer and improved? Think about how your relationship would be having the new and improved spouse.*

Husbands and Wives: Evaluate your marriage, what can you sacrifice temporarily to bring back the love, passion and the bond? What can you sacrifice to rediscover each other? When was the last time you did an act of love because it came from the heart and not to gain something? What is hindering you from taking your relationship to next level?

The Blame Game

"When difficulties arise, when conflicts happen there are numerous ways you can act. The way you decide to act will have a reaction, which is either a positive reaction or negative reaction. When conflict does happen the most common action a person does is deflect and deter by pointing their finger at the other person involved and taking no responsibility or having no accountability in the argument that occurred. You always play the victim and in your head you are always innocent while the other person is always at fault."

During those three months of non-sexual contact we discussed everything. But one of the most important talks we had was about fighting, arguing, disagreements and if we were to get upset with each other. We discussed that we were not perfect, so disagreements would happen. But with that being said, we do control how we act and what comes out of our mouths. There is no excuse for disrespect. We both agreed. As the days went on, our first test finally presented itself. I'll explain.

We agreed to watch our niece and nephew for the weekend. I told Mary previously before we committed, to hang out with her homegirls, go shopping, eat lunch and just have a girls day out. Well that weekend we accidentally double booked ourselves. I wanted Mary to enjoy her girl time so I said to her, "Baby I got it covered, I'll watch our niece and nephew and you just enjoy yourself with your friends as planned." Saturday morning arrives, the day of babysitting. I am super exhausted from work. I'm laying in bed and just like that the sandman gives me a left hook knocking me out, putting me in dreamland snoring. While I'm knocked out the referee wakes me up.

Well if you can't put two and two together the referee was Mary lol. Mary wakes me up and asks me to watch our niece and nephew while she gets dressed to go out. I said to her in a groggy voice, "I'm already watching the kids when you leave I don't want to right now. I'm tired." she said, "How am I supposed to get dressed while I'm watching them." I replied by saying, "Baby just do it. Come on. I'm already going to watch them when you leave." She just left the room without responding and I could tell she was upset.

My heart convicted me. I hopped out of bed and said to her that I would watch the kids and she responded by saying she would watch them and that it was fine. The atmosphere in the room was not right. So I just told her to get dressed and I got the kids. And before she could respond I took the kids downstairs. After she was done getting dressed I told her she looked nice and I apologized, she apologized as well. As she was headed to her destination she called me on the phone and apologized again and so did I.

When she came home everything was normal and lovey dovey like always. As the night was ending we were in bed and my heart convicted me again. This time around in our new relationship I'm always listening to my heart. I'm being more communicative and vulnerable. The macho man way and the saying of 'a man is not supposed to share their feelings' was out the window for me. Holding things in and not saying what's on my heart only created animosities. I refused to do the same things of the past.

I followed my heart and I told her that we needed to talk about earlier that day. Even though we apologized to each other I felt it wasn't resolved. I said to her, "I want to try something new but first I want to reassure you that I will always have your best interest in my heart. I love you, and I'm not in the business to attack and put down my wife."

After I laid out my disclaimer, I got into the disagreement we had earlier. I explained that in the past we would point fingers at each other and play the blame game of why it was the other person's fault and who was right and who was wrong. When we did it that way we both got offended. So this time what I want to do was to point the finger at ourselves and tell each other what could we have done differently to either prevent the disagreement from happening or by taking accountability for the disagreement 100%. That way if I point the finger at myself you won't get offended and if you point the finger at yourself I won't get offended.

I went first. I said, "I apologize for my actions and I feel if I would have sacrificed my sleep for 30 minutes and watched our niece and nephew none of this would have happened. I should have put myself in your shoes and realized that it is hard to get dressed and watch out for the safety of the kids at the same time. My lack of helping you out when you needed my help is the reason why you acted the way you did. I take full responsibility for the disagreement."

When I was done, she responded by saying, "I apologize. If I put myself in your shoes I would have realized you were extremely tired after work. I realized you were sacrificing the whole day babysitting the kids so I could have girl time with my friends. So if I would have just sacrificed and watched the kids and got dressed at the same time, no disagreement would of occurred." She ended by taking 100% blame for the disagreement.

We both felt good, fulfilled and liked how we handled our first disagreement. We both took ownership of what we did without blaming the other person. The respect was there, the love was there and we didn't have to have dessert to make up for the dinner. Lol *The same 3 course meal'* is now broken and nonexistent in our new marriage. The mind frame of everybody fights is now nonexistent in our marriage. We are creating our own path of how our marriage goes now and not going with the norm.

Another Situation

Mary was at work and she sent me about four text messages throughout her day at work. She sent me more but I'm only going to talk about the four important ones. Each of the four text messages was a 'Hey how's it going?' How was your day? And in each of the four responses the text message I sent was 'I'm super frustrated.' 'I'm frustrated.' And 'I'm stressed out because of work.' When Mary comes home I'm expecting a big hug as usual, but instead I received a short hug and then she hurriedly went into the kitchen to make dinner. With the unusual behavior I assumed she was mad and I asked her what was wrong? She responded by saying she wasn't mad. She explained that I had a mad tone when she came home and she just wanted to cook dinner to avoid me. I told her that I purposely told myself to be nice to you and not take out my stressful day on you.

Then it clicked and it hit me like lightning. I immediately told her I was sorry, and I pointed the finger at myself saying that the text messages I was sending you about me being frustrated created the mood and the tense atmosphere. I further explained that next time I won't go on and on about me being frustrated because those me being frustrated texts put you in the mind frame that I was upset. And I ended it by again taking full responsibility by creating the tense atmosphere. Even though Mary didn't have to, she pointed the finger at herself saying that if she didn't assume I was mad, probably everything would have been normal. She also said she should have judged me on my actions when she came through the door and not based on the text messages. And she ended it by saying she was sorry.

  We no longer play the blame game in our household. We now take full responsibility for our actions by pointing the finger at ourselves. We learned from the past that when we point fingers at each other, our guards immediately go up, we get offended and start finding ways to make the other person look bad and in return we start to build animosities towards each other.

  Our new way works for us because we are accountable, apologetic and we explain how we could have avoided the disagreement or argument by pointing the finger at ourselves. The result was we don't offend each other nor create animosities.

****Time To Reflect****

Reflect to the arguments and disagreements you may had. Nobody is perfect so disagreements will happen but they can happen respectfully with a respectful tone. Imagine how your relationship would be if you pointed the finger at yourself and not blame the other.

Husbands and Wives: Think about the past and how the arguments went. Think about how you pointed the finger at each other and blamed each other. How did it feel to get blamed? Did you get offended, mad, and say things to get back at your partner? Try to disagree in a new way. Point the finger at yourself from here on out. Think about pointing the finger at yourself and the positive impact it will have on your relationship. The old way of arguing doesn't work. Rewire your brain and protect your partner of any ill will feelings they can create by taking full responsibility.

Watering the Plant

"When a plant is watered the plant grows. If you don't water the plant it dies. The plant is symbolic to the husband and wife. Therefore if you continuously water your spouse and vice versa then your marriage will grow. If you continuously study and learn your spouse it will flourish. If you choose not to continuously water your spouse's plant then just like the plant it will shrivel up and die."

I'm not trying to be a teacher, preacher, marriage counselor or a therapist. I consider myself a hood historian sharing my marriage experiences that worked for me. I say I'm a historian because I studied the history of my marriage, learned from it and began to do the complete opposite so I could get different results. *"Genius Right?"* The way Mary and I did marriage before killed our marriage. By now our marriage was reborn and I made a commitment to myself to never let my marriage shrivel up or get complacent.

I also made a commitment to appreciate what I have in Mary, by not only telling her I love her but by showing her as well. Because love is an action word so even if I don't verbally say I love you, she will still feel 100% loved. But me being the man that I am I do both. Verbal and by action. Holla!!!

I love my wife and I want my marriage to flourish. So every day I water Mary's plant, I water her mind, body and soul, physically, emotionally, and mentally.

Watering the plant does not have to be rocket science or complicated. To me it's simple. You know how you literally take a bottle of water and pour it into a plant? Yes it's that simple. Some examples of how I water Mary's plant is by just taking time out of my day to talk to her about how her day was. Maybe give her a massage, cook dinner for her, chill on the couch and watch her favorite tv shows with her, even if I don't even like the shows. I left 'good morning' notes in her car, surprised her with breakfast in bed, filled up her gas tank when she was on empty and taking just five minutes out of the day to tell her how much she meant to me. Everyday doesn't have to be explosive or magical. But I made a commitment to myself to do something every day. Some days more than others. But every day I take the bottle of water and pour it into my plant.

I'm very strict with myself because I figure if I don't water her plant daily then it will become un-watered weekly, monthly, then yearly and eventually the marriage would die or be in a vegetable state (complacent). So Mary and I water each other's plants daily so there will be no complacency in the marriage. The reason why we do this is so we both feel wanted, loved and special and to let the other person know that they see each other and recognize their worth.

Studying and learning each other daily is another way to water each other's plant. I love learning new things about Mary that she doesn't even know about herself. When I apply what I learned and see her reactions, body language, and see her feel loved, it excites me. Sometimes we ourselves don't even know what we want or need to make us feel loved. For example, I didn't know I wanted to be hugged with passion after not seeing Mary all day from her being at work until I received my first lackadaisical hug. I didn't like that feeling and it brought back old memories. So Mary studied and learned that about me so now when she sees me, she hugs me with meaning and passion because she knows that's how my plant gets watered.

Back in the past we unknowingly would study and learn each other for the wrong reason. We would study each other's weaknesses and what pissed us off and ended up using it against each other to either start an argument or to use as a low blow. Even though we were super young, it's still not an excuse. But now the vibe is totally different in the household.

I learned that Mary likes surprises and sacrifices of love. When I say surprises, I don't mean gifts. The surprises I am talking about is doing things unexpected. For example, if she was watching her ratchet reality tv shows, lol, I would lay in bed with her and watch it with her. And if it's before I go to work she would insist I take a nap before work and I let her know by saying, "Baby today is about you. I'm going to watch your shows with you even though I can't stand those shows I'm going to sacrifice my nap before work to just bond with you." That small act of love means the world to her.

Mary constantly is learning about me and I realized that when I do something for her and all she tells me is thank you, I unknowingly get into my diva stage where I need a snicker bar to snap out of my diva-ness. LOL. In the past if she responds with just a thank you, I act like a diva, get into my feelings and I feel like she didn't appreciate it. Then she will have to defend herself and say she did appreciate it. I guess she has been studying the past too. Because now when I do acts of love or do anything for her she goes overboard, is super thankful and breaks down how she felt at that moment, how she felt surprised and how thankful she was. She doesn't just pat me on the back. She paaaaaaaaaaats me on the back. She knows from learning that I like to be praised and to be shown massive amounts of appreciation. So now Mary always has the pom poms out to show her appreciation, because I'm her husband, she is my biggest cheerleader and she knows how to my water my plant so I can feel loved. With us both watering each other's plants, our plants began to flourish.

Time To Reflect

Husbands and Wives: Think about your past and ask yourselves, have you been watering each other's plant? Is your marriage complacent? Think about your plant getting watered daily and vice versa? With daily watering do you think that would make you feel special, loved and appreciated? From here on out make a conscious decision to study, learn each other and implement what you learned by applying it and never stop. Whether big or small water the plant daily so it will flourish.

24 hours to Live

A question we all have asked ourselves and contemplated about. If you had 24 hours to live what would you do? Those 24 hours wouldn't be like any other 24 hours you ever lived. You will make the most out of every single second, every single minute and every single hour of the day. A normal 24 hours, you would usually put off what you can do today because you know there is always a tomorrow. But your last 24 hours YOU WOULD ENJOY, CHERISH, APPRECIATE, AND YOU WOULD MAKE IT MEMORABLE.

(A letter I wrote Mary after our rebirth)
Mary,

Love me, treat me, cater to me, cherish me, appreciate me, embrace me, adore me, and enjoy me like it's my last day on this earth. Now that right there is super deep. When people pass away or when people and friendships fall apart we all reflect on the things we could have done differently. But with you and I, we don't have to wait until divorce to say I wish I could have done this different or I wish I could have done more. If we apply this '24 hours to live' phrase to our marriage, then we will flourish. Love me like the doctor just told you privately that I only have 24 hours to live. If I had 24 hours to live and you truly love me, would you just go with the flow and be nonchalant with me for those 24 hours? Would you kiss me lazily? Hug me with no passion behind it? The answer is 'NO'. If you love me with all your heart and the doc told you I had 24 hours to live, you would hug me with so much passion, kiss me with so much love, engage with me with so much attention. You would appreciate my last hours because you know that this will be the last time you would ever be in my presence. You would want to capture that moment and hold onto that memory the rest of your life having no regrets. EVERY DAY SHOULD BE LIKE THIS.

  Baby I promise I tell myself this when I wake up in the morning to start my day. Baby if I knew this was going to be your last 24 hours, I would want to make a lasting impression on your mind, body, heart and soul, physically, emotionally, mentally, and spiritually. I would kiss you like you have never been kissed before. I would hug you, talk to you, appreciate and cherish you like I would never get a chance to again. I would cater to you and act so loving, pouring my heart out to you. I would make love to you with so much passion, holding you, and letting my heartbeat next to yours so I can feel at one with you. I would take every second of those 24 hours to just cherish you because once you are gone, all I have are those lasting memories. And I can honestly say I captured her last 24 hours with no regrets.

Time to Reflect

This chapter really needs no explaining. How would you feel if your partner was no longer alive? Really embed yourself in this chapter and say to yourself, "Wow the doctor just told me my spouse has 24 hours to live." Reflect and ponder on this thought.

Husbands and Wives: Take a look at the way you did things in the past. Would you want the last impression your spouse has of you to be how you treated them in the past? Think about your spouse only having 24 hours to live. What would you do in those 24 hours to show your spouse that you love and appreciate them? Fantasize about how you would play out those 24 hours. Can you commit yourself to live life with each other like you only have 24 hours to live?

The Fat Lady Has Sung

The ending, the conclusion, the finale, the completion; A term used to emphasize when something is finished.

May 19, 2011 was the day my marriage was rebirthed, reborn, and resurrected. May 19th was the day I began to love Mary with a new heart and see her through new eyes. When I first met Mary in 2004 there was not a single doubt in my heart, my love for her. Prior to our first date, we spent numerous hours on the phone building a connection deeper than the physical. The chemistry was so strong and so beautiful that when our first date ended no lie I wanted to ask her to marry me.

My heart told me she was the one, and the one she was. My heart has never lied to me, over the months and years together, she proved her worth and proved she was my *'Ride or Die'* and that's why I got down on one knee and asked her to marry me and have my last name. Throughout time we lost our way during *'The Same 3 course Meal'* which lead to the *'12th Round Knockout.'* When I was defeated, I *'Trusted the Process'* and during the process I looked at my reflection. And I'm telling you *'The Mirror Doesn't Lie.'* I saw my ugliness and the animosities I held and from the bottom of my heart I apologized. When I was defeated, destroyed and my whole confidence was crumbled, God revealed my self-worth and beauty and through that revelation *'The New Twin Towers'* was rebuilt.

During the process I reminisced back to *'Cuffing Season'* and saw the reason why she fell in love with me. During those three days of no contact visually or verbally, I wrote expressing my feelings, thoughts and emotions and with my mind, heart, body, soul and myself all in agreement it was confirmation that Mary is all I ever needed in this world. She was my heartbeat and had always been the missing piece to my puzzle which completes me and with that our marriage had *'The Rebirth'.*

May 19, 2011 when I walked through those doors we hugged like it was our first time. I then felt *'Fasting'* was necessary to take our marriage to new heights and during the fasting we relearned, rediscovered ourselves and I got my best friend back. We looked back at our past and although our love was never in question, we studied the past so in the future we wouldn't make the same mistakes. Seven years later we are still *'Watering the Plant'*. We still don't play *'The Blame Game'* and most importantly we are still operating like we only have *'24 Hours to Live'*. Our marriage has flourished!! From May 19, 2011 until now 2018 we have 2 kids - one daughter that's 6 years old and one son that is 2 years old and with the new added responsibilities we are still staying young in love.

** *Time to Reflect* **

Husbands and Wives: You can lead a horse to the water but you can't make the horse drink. With that being said, this is my story, and what I learned and what works for Mary and I. I was compelled to write this book for the people that were at the 50/50 point in their relationship and wanted to give it one more try. Did this book help you out? You must honestly ask and answer that yourself. At the end of the day this book was written to help you rediscover yourself. To remind yourself of the beautiful person you once were and how you can be that again. I also wrote this book so you can see your spouse with new eyes and love your spouse with a new heart. The choice is yours. Sit down and have a long conversation with your spouse. Have the realest talk ever and figure out what you guys will do and how things will be different from the past. Email me at BeforeItsToooLate@hotmail.com and keep me posted. Peace Out 😛

Words From My Wife

To My Honey Buns,

First of All I want to say WOW!!! Never in a million years would I have ever thought you would write a book, let alone a book about our journey to endless love. Ever since I met you 14 years ago till now, you always put me on a pedestal, surprised me, adored me, and most importantly shown me that I meant the world to you. Hubby I truly love you with all of my heart, you are the most loving, sweetest, and I can't forget the sexiest man I ever met LMAO (it's true) But seriously ever since you entered my life you changed my world. You are all I ever wanted without any doubt. I can't believe we were kids when we first met. We didn't have a clue what we were doing back then but all we knew is that we loved each other. So many sacrifices you made for me, so many memories and so many laughs we shared and continue to share. You cater to ALL my needs and you always provided for me. You are so romantic, you have a beautiful mind, and the biggest heart. But the icing on the cake is your silly-ness, and goofy-ness. I'm honestly living a real life fairy tale. I'm not going to lie you can be a PAIN IN THE ASS at times, but YOU ARE MY PAIN IN THE ASS. Before our rebirth my life was complete. You were my dream man. I thought my life couldn't get any better. But wow, I must say that our relationship really took to new heights after May 19th. I don't know what you went through those three days when we didn't talk, but I thank God from the bottom of my heart. We were great back then but now we are reaching new levels daily. When I have a diva attitude you manage to always calm me down, you understand me, you never judge me and you always let me be myself. I love the man you were to the man you have become. Now, 7 years later after our rebirth and having 2 kids with you. I can't get enough of your love. I love you always.

Your adoring wife,
Mary Williams

www.ingramcontent.com/pod-product-compliance
Lightning Source LLC
Chambersburg PA
CBHW021410290426
44108CB00010B/469